The Nature Kid's Guide to
SPIDERS

DAVID ANDERSON

LP Media Inc. Publishing
Text copyright © 2026 by LP Media Inc.
All rights reserved.

For information address LP Media Inc. Publishing,
30012 Variolite St NW, Princeton MN 55371
www.lpmedia.org

Publication Data

Spiders
The Nature Kid's Guide to Spiders — First edition.

Summary: "Learn all about Spiders, the Nature Kid Way"
— Provided by publisher.

ISBN: 979-8-89818-181-9

[1. Spiders – Non-Fiction] I. Title.

Title: The Nature Kid's Guide to Spiders

CONTENTS

SPIDER SECRETS

Some spiders can survive being frozen solid in ice and wake up perfectly fine when they thaw out!

Whoosh! A tiny spider crawls on its silk web.

Spiders live all over the world. You can find them in forests, deserts, and even your own backyard. There are more than 45,000 kinds of spiders!

Spiders are not insects. They have eight legs, not six. They belong to a group called **arachnids**, which also includes scorpions and ticks.

Most spiders are shy and small. They hide under rocks and leaves. But each one has amazing skills to find food and stay safe. These eight-legged hunters are full of surprises.

SPIDER SENSES

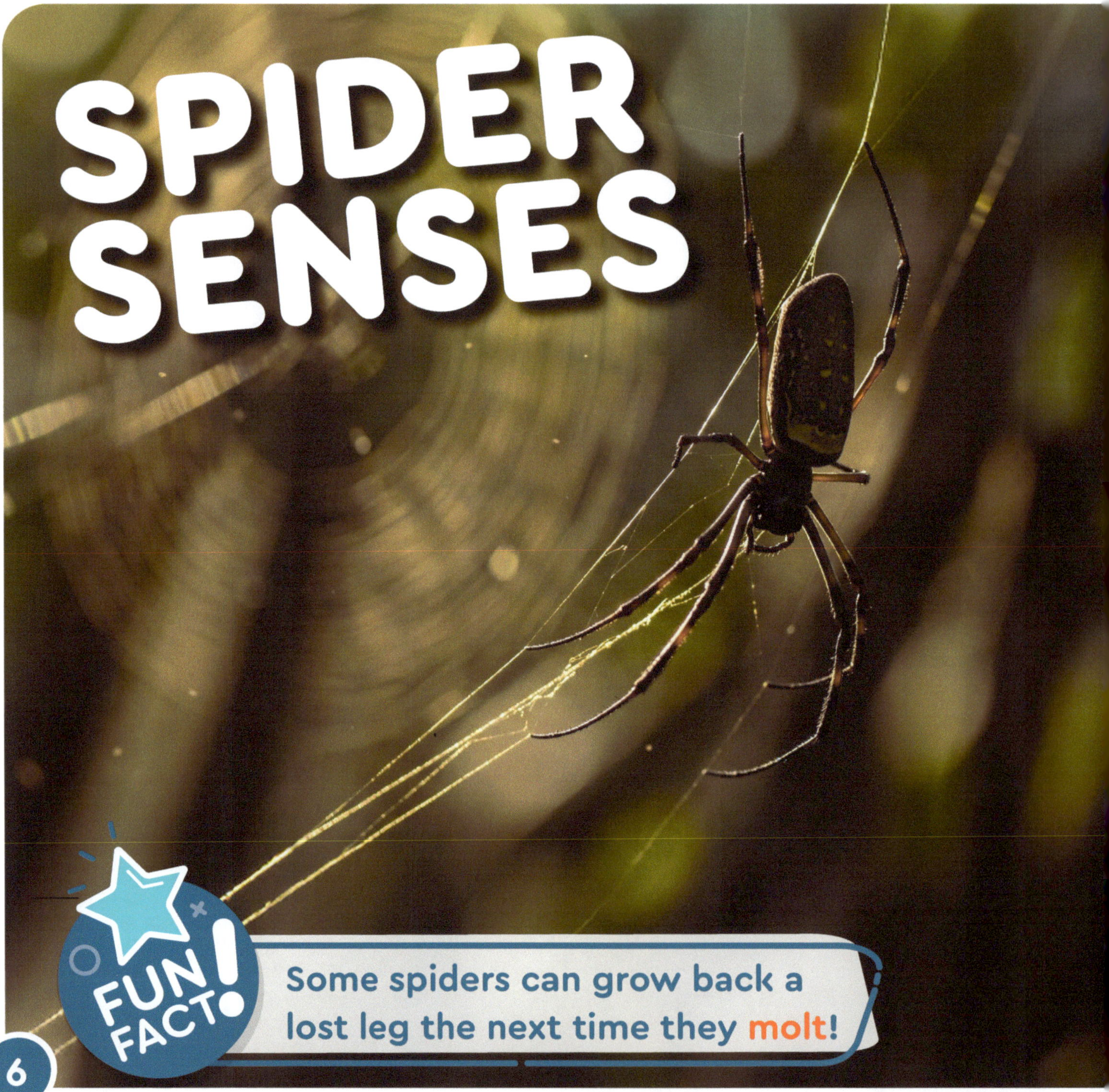

Some spiders can grow back a lost leg the next time they **molt**!

Spin, twist! Eight tiny legs spin a web. It's trying to catch lunch!

A spider's body has two main parts. The front part holds the brain, eyes, and fangs. The back part makes silk.

Most spiders have eight eyes! Some can see very well. Others can only tell light from dark. Tiny hairs cover their legs and help them feel the world around them.

Those hairs pick up small shakes in the air. This tells a spider when prey is close. It also warns them when danger is near. A spider's body is built for survival.

SPINNING SILK

Zing! A silk line shoots out and sticks to a branch.

Spider silk comes from spinnerets on a spider's belly. These are like tiny tubes that push out liquid. The liquid hardens into silk as it hits the air.

Silk is incredibly strong for its size. It can stretch up to four times its length without breaking! Spiders use it to build webs, wrap food, and make egg sacs.

Not all webs look the same. Some are round and flat. Others look like funnels or messy tangles. Each spider builds the web that works best for catching its favorite prey.

HUNTING TACTICS

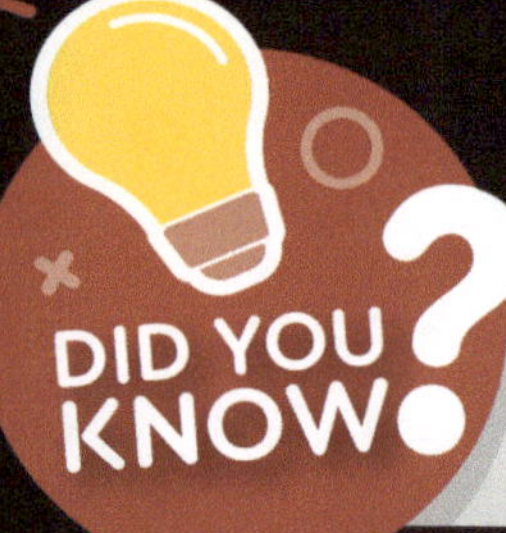

Most spider venom is harmless to people, but it is deadly to bugs!

Snap! A fly gets trapped and shakes the web. The black widow crawls to get it!

Spiders are skilled hunters. Some spin webs and wait for bugs to fly in. Others chase their prey across the ground.

When a spider catches food, it bites with its fangs. Most spiders have venom that stops their prey from moving. Then they wrap the meal up in silk to save for later.

Some spiders spit sticky goo. Others set traps with silk trip lines. A few even throw tiny webs like nets! Each spider has its own clever way to catch a meal.

TERRIFIC TARANTULAS

Thud! A big, furry tarantula drops down from a log.

Tarantulas are some of the biggest spiders in the world. The largest can be as wide as a dinner plate! Most live in warm places like deserts and rain forests.

These hairy spiders do not spin webs to catch food. They hunt at night instead. They creep along the ground and pounce on bugs, frogs, and even small mice.

Tarantulas may look scary, but they are gentle giants. They would rather run and hide than bite. Some live for over 20 years, making them one of the longest-lived spiders on Earth.

WIDOW'S WARNING

Twang! A black widow plucks a silk thread on its messy web.

Black widows are small but famous. You can spot one by the red shape on its belly. That bright mark says, "Stay away!"

Black widows build messy webs in dark places. They like garages, sheds, and wood piles. These shy spiders hide during the day and only bite when scared.

Their venom is strong — 15 times stronger than a rattlesnake's! But bites are very rare. Black widows try hard to stay out of sight and away from people.

JUMPING JEWELS

DID YOU KNOW?

There are more than 6,000 kinds of jumping spiders — that's more than any other spider family!

Boing! A tiny jumping spider leaps into the air!

Jumping spiders are tiny but mighty. They do not use webs to catch prey. Instead, they leap through the air to grab bugs!

These small spiders have big front eyes that see very well. They can spot a bug from 8 inches away. Then they stalk it slowly, like a little cat hunting a mouse.

Jumping spiders come in many bright colors. Some shimmer with green, blue, or orange. They are one of the most colorful spider groups, and one of the smartest too.

SPIRAL SPINNERS

Some orb weaver webs have a bright zigzag pattern that may keep birds from flying through!

Swish! An orb weaver spins a web as round as a wheel.

Orb weavers build the webs you see in storybooks. Each web has a spiral of sticky silk. It takes about one hour to build, but the spider works fast.

These spiders often sit in the center of their web and wait. When a bug flies in and gets stuck, the spider feels the web shake. Then it rushes over to grab its meal.

Many orb weavers take down their web each morning. They eat the old silk to recycle it. Then they spin a fresh web at night, ready for another hunt.

SPRINTING SPIDERS

DID YOU KNOW?

Zoom! A wolf spider races across the ground after a bug.

Wolf spiders are fast and strong. They do not sit in webs and wait. Instead, they run down their prey like tiny wolves chasing a rabbit.

These brown and gray spiders live on the ground. They hide under rocks, leaves, and logs during the day. Their colors help them blend in perfectly with the dirt.

Wolf spider moms are amazing parents. They carry their babies on their backs! Hundreds of tiny spiders ride along until they are big enough to hunt on their own.

TRAPDOOR TRICKS

Crash! A trapdoor spider bursts from its hidden hole.

Trapdoor spiders dig **burrows** in the ground. They cover the top with a lid made of silk and dirt. The lid looks just like the ground around it. It is a perfect disguise.

The spider waits inside with the door shut tight. When a bug walks by, it feels the tiny footsteps through the ground. Then it pops out, grabs the bug, and pulls it inside in a flash.

These patient spiders can live in the same burrow for many years. Some burrows are over 20 years old! They are clever hunters that never need to chase their food.

FUNNEL FURY

DID YOU KNOW?
The Sydney funnel web spider has fangs strong enough to bite through a leather shoe!

Rustle! A funnel web spider darts into its silk tunnel.

The Sydney funnel web is one of the most dangerous spiders in the world. Its venom can make a person very sick in just 15 minutes.

These spiders live in dark, damp places in Australia. Some dig burrows near rocks or tree roots. They spin webs shaped like funnels (that's how they got their name!), with a wide opening and a narrow tunnel to hide in.

When a bug steps on the web, the spider feels it right away. It races out of the funnel and grabs its meal in a flash. Then it drags the prey back into its tunnel to eat.

SILK SHIMMER

Golden silk spider webs can last for years without breaking — even in rain and wind!

Whir! A golden silk spider spins a web that shines like gold.

Golden silk spiders build some of the biggest webs in the world. Some stretch over six feet wide! Their silk shines in the sun like tiny gold threads.

Golden silk spiders live in warm forests. They hang in the middle of their huge webs and wait for bugs. Their webs are so strong that small birds sometimes get caught by mistake.

People have used golden silk to make cloth for hundreds of years. This silk is very tough and hard to break. It is one of the strongest natural threads in the world.

CRAB CAMO

FUN FACT!
A crab spider can wait perfectly still on the same flower for days, just waiting for the right meal!

28

Pop! A crab spider appears from inside a yellow flower.

Crab spiders look a lot like tiny crabs. They hold their front legs out to the sides. They can even walk sideways, just like a crab on the beach!

These spiders do not chase their food. They sit on flowers and wait. When a bee or butterfly lands to drink nectar, the crab spider grabs it fast.

Some crab spiders can change their color over a few days. They turn white or yellow to match the flower they sit on. This clever trick helps them hide from both prey and enemies.

DANCING DAZZLERS

FUN FACT!

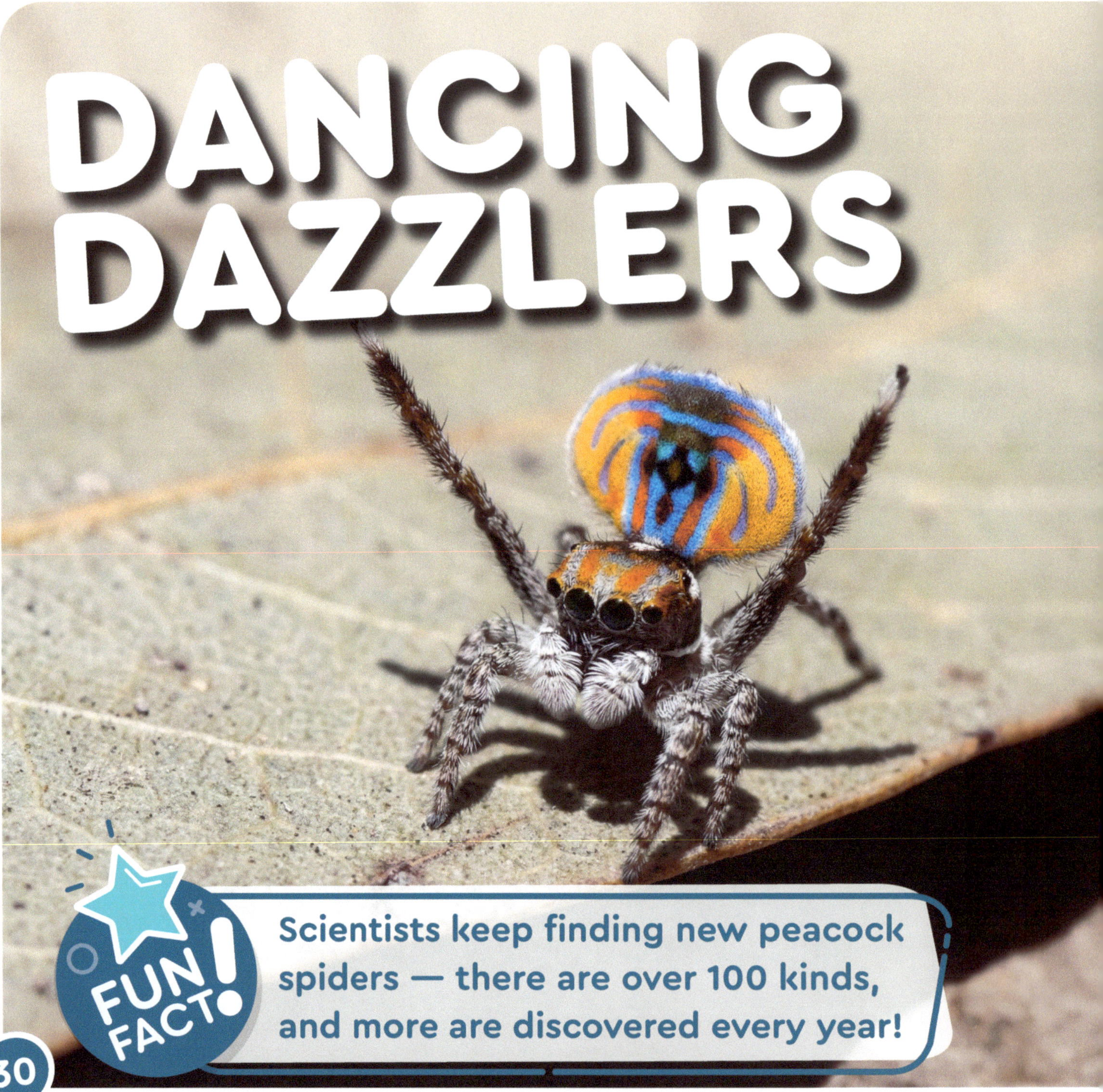

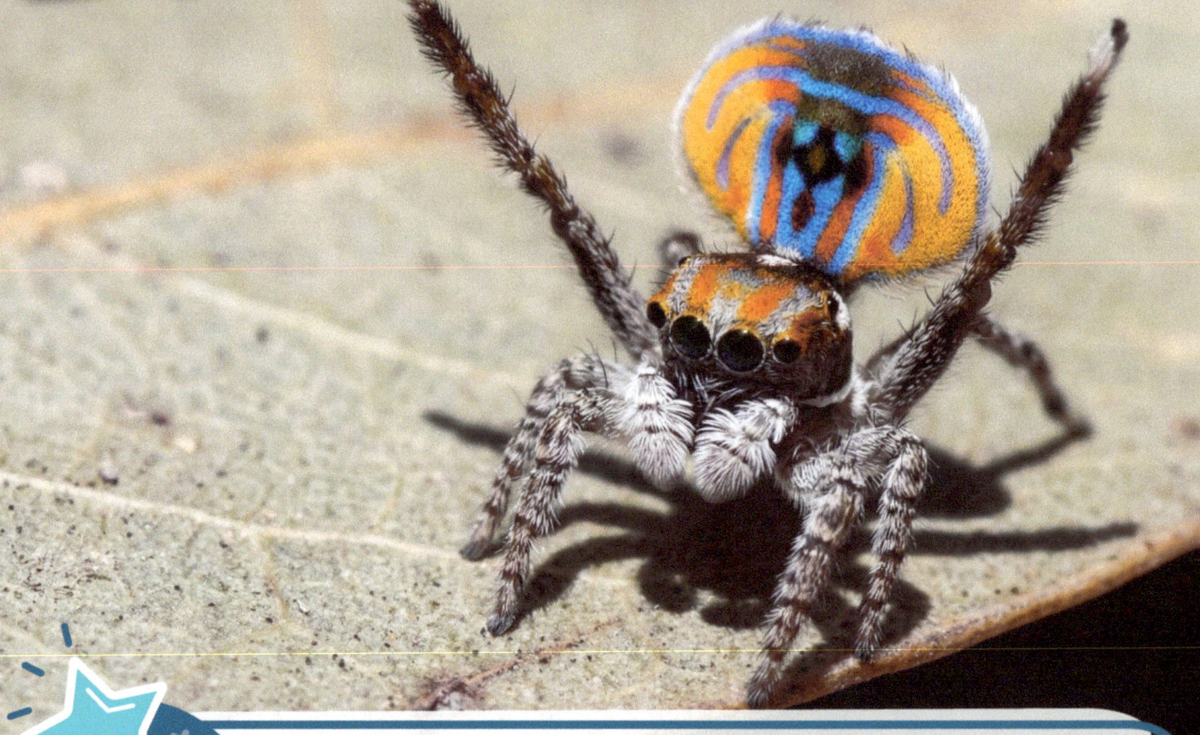

Scientists keep finding new peacock spiders — there are over 100 kinds, and more are discovered every year!

Tap, tap! A peacock spider starts to dance and show off.

Peacock spiders are some of the flashiest spiders alive. Males have bright belly flaps covered with bold patterns. They lift these flaps high to show off their dazzling colors.

To win a mate, the male does a dance. He waves his legs, shakes his body, and even vibrates! If the female likes the show, she lets him come close.

Peacock spiders are a kind of jumping spider. They live in Australia and are very tiny – only as big as a grain of rice! But what they lack in size, they make up for in style and dance moves.

BUBBLE BUILDER

32

Blub! A diving bell spider crawls out of its under water air bubble!

The diving bell spider is the only spider on earth that lives under water. It breathes air, just like you. But it spends most of its life in ponds and streams.

This clever spider builds a tiny air bubble with silk. It swims to the surface to grab fresh air and brings it back down. The bubble works like a small room where the spider rests, eats, and even raises babies.

Diving bell spiders catch water bugs and tiny fish. They are amazing swimmers with legs covered in tiny hairs that trap air. No other spider lives quite like this one.

HUGE HUNTSMAN

DID YOU KNOW?

34

Skitter! A giant huntsman spider races across the wall.

Huntsman spiders have legs that stretch very wide. Their legs can spread wider than this book — up to 12 inches across! They live in warm places like Australia and Asia.

These spiders are super fast runners. They do not build webs at all. Instead, they chase prey along walls, trees, and rocks at top speed.

Huntsman spiders sometimes sneak into homes and surprise people. They look scary, but they are harmless. They even help by eating bugs like cockroaches and moths.

In Australia, some people let them live in their house. They like that they eat all the bugs!

SECRET HELPERS

Munch! A spider catches a pesky fly on a deck railing.

Spiders are some of nature's best bug catchers. They eat billions of insects every year! Without spiders, our homes, gardens, and parks would be crawling with way more bugs!

Farmers love spiders because they gobble up **pests** that damage crops. Scientists study spider silk to create new super-strong materials. Others study venom to help make medicines that save lives.

Most spiders want nothing to do with people. If you spot one, just let it be. That little spider is already hard at work keeping bugs away from you!

SPIDER HUNTING
FUN FACT!
Spiders live on every **continent** in the world except icy Antarctica!

Swoop! A spider glides down from a branch on a silk thread.

Spiders might seem scary, but finding them is actually a blast! Check under rocks, peek in garage corners, or look along fences and bushes. Early morning is the best time to spot webs because the dew makes them sparkle.

If you find a spider, do not touch it. Just crouch down and watch how it moves, builds, and catches its food. A magnifying glass makes the details even more amazing.

Snap pictures or draw the spiders you find. Write down where you spotted them and what they were doing. You might be surprised how many kinds live right in your own backyard!

GLOSSARY

arachnid
An animal with eight legs
and two body parts

burrow
A hole or tunnel dug by an
animal in the ground

continent
One of the seven large
land areas on Earth

molt
When an animal sheds its
old skin to grow

pests
Bugs that cause problems
for people or plants